"…*not here, present elsewhere*…"

My messages from Michael

Mary O'Farrell

ISBN 979-8-88751-575-5 (paperback)
ISBN 979-8-88751-576-2 (digital)

Christian Faith Publishing
832 Park Avenue
Meadville, PA 16335
www.christianfaithpublishing.com

Printed in the United States of America

Introduction

I have always loved books and, in particular, used books. I am a very curious person, and, in the late 1970s, I came across a book that would change my life. The book was called *Life After Death* and was described as "the book that shatters every myth about mortality." It was published in Great Britain in 1975 by Robert Hale Limited and written by a man named Neville Randall. Even then, though only a few years old, the book was somewhat worn as it had obviously been sold and resold and read and reread a number of times. Since it has been in my hands, it has once again been read and reread.

The book is a compendium of twenty-one transcripts, out of over five hundred recordings, of word-for-word conversations between a famous British psychic medium named Ena Twigg and people who have passed to the other side. This is the book that started me on my quest of almost fifty years to learn all I could about life after death and especially near-death experiences, which continues to this day.

The word *death* raises in the minds of people the finality of life as they know it, without any recourse. During the course of our lives, we will all lose a loved one, if we live long enough. What we experience when we lose someone is the excruciating loss of the physical person. What we need to know is that, while they are not here physically, they still do exist. This fact was brought home to me when I read *Beyond the Light* by P. M. H. Atwater—in particular, on the last page of the introduction, where she wrote, "The Aramaic word for death translates *'not here, present elsewhere.'* This ancient concept of death best describes the near-death experience and what happens to those who go through it"; hence, the title of this book. Our loved

"

ones are present—elsewhere—and are still able to connect with us if only we take the time to ask, wait, listen, and watch for the signs they are sending to let us know they are still a part of our lives.

I am a firm believer that things happen for a reason. There are far fewer random occurrences in life than one might like to believe. That you have picked up this book is not a random occurrence. You were led to pick it up for a reason. That reason may not be obvious today, but I believe it will show itself in the weeks or months, or perhaps even years, ahead.

I hope that this book will be of help to you or, perhaps, someone you know, and that my messages from Michael will impart an uplifting feeling to all who are not afraid to question, research, and explore "the other side."

Chapter 1

As with all stories, it is always best to start at the beginning, which is what I will do here.

The beginning was a cold but sunny day near the end of November in 1964. I think the date was the twenty-fourth, about six weeks prior to my eighteenth birthday. At that time I was working as secretary to the Deputy Director of what was then called the Combines Investigation Branch, with a staff of about sixty people, in the Canadian Federal Department of Justice.

By then I had been working for about eighteen months and had enjoyed the work tremendously. Because of my age, most of the officers, as those above the support and administrative levels were called, were old enough to be my father, and, for most of the time, the atmosphere in the Branch was rather staid, except during the summer months when it became exciting. During these months, the Department would hire university students on summer break who were studying to become lawyers, economists, and statisticians to help with the cases that the officers in the Branch were investigating and to give the students some work experience in the "real world." Come the fall, the students would all return to their various universities, and the atmosphere in the office would return to normal.

My office was next to that of the Deputy Director on the seventh floor of the Justice Building on Wellington Street with its window facing west, allowing a beautiful view of the setting sun. Around four o'clock on that particular day, I was looking out the window and thinking that perhaps it was time for me to consider a transfer to another government department where there might be some young people I could meet and with whom I could make friends. I was thinking of the Department of External Affairs, as at least there, if nothing else, I might get to do some traveling.

Suddenly, I heard my name being called and turned to find a vision at my office door—a man with the bluest eyes I had ever seen and a smile that simply lit up the room. He was being introduced to me as the new officer who would be reporting to my boss, the Deputy Director. To say that I was completely smitten would be a huge understatement. His name was Michael, and from that second onward, he was the only one with whom I wanted and would, in fact, be so very, very lucky to spend the rest of my life.

As luck would have it, he was just finishing up research he had been doing during the summer months for an economist named Dr. Eugene Forsey who was writing a book about the history of the labor movement in Canada. The research Michael was doing involved his reading historical documents on microfiche rolls and making notes to provide to Dr. Forsey. As he was now a full-time employee of the Department of Justice, Michael would need to do the research after work, and he would no longer have the time to write the notes out by hand.

The Combines Investigation Branch, like many other government agencies, had its own microfiche reader, as well as a stenographic typing pool. Given these amenities, Michael decided to ask the Deputy Director if he could hire a stenographer to work at night to take dictation of the information from the rolls and then type it up for him. That way he could complete his work for Dr. Forsey in the time stipulated by his research contract.

Upon hearing his request, the Deputy Director said that he definitely could *not* hire anyone from the steno pool or there would be no work done there at all by the girls because of all the chattering that would ensue, but he gave Michael permission to ask me, and, if I was willing, the Deputy Director said that it would be fine with him. Needless to say, I readily agreed, provided he take me to supper each day as I would not have time to go home, change, and return to the office. He liked this idea and agreed to my terms. The first supper we had was at the Bel Air restaurant on Queen Street. It was a combination pizza, something I had never eaten before and have loved ever since.

It took several months for Michael to finish with the microfiche rolls. After the work ended, Michael and I started dating, and the rest, as the saying goes, is history. We dated throughout 1965 and were married at 10:00 a.m. on Saturday, May 7, 1966, in Sainte Jeanne d'Arc Roman Catholic Church.

As I have often told my friends, if anyone tells them that there is no such thing as "love at first sight," have them talk to me.

Chapter 2

I'll now tell you a bit about my Michael and why he was—and still is, even though he is gone—the remarkable man I love so dearly.

During his youth, Michael delivered a newspaper route and, also in the evening after school, using his bicycle, he delivered prescription medications for a local pharmacy. Because Michael's father had been ill and unable to work for a number of years, his mother had taken over supporting the family by cleaning offices at night. Such menial jobs do not provide much in the way of salary, so money was scarce, and anything that Michael needed beyond the bare necessities, he had to buy for himself. Michael's bicycle had been a secondhand one, and, with all the deliveries he was making, especially during the winter months through the ice, snow, and slush, the bicycle was beginning to show a lot of wear. So he decided it was time to invest in a new one.

Michael kept all his money from both jobs in an old shoebox. The amount of savings was starting to mount up, and he decided that it would be safer to keep it in a savings account in the bank. So he took himself off to the local bank to open one. The teller he met at the counter asked him his age and told him that he was not old enough to have a bank account. Michael persisted and insisted he wanted to talk to the bank manager. Having a boy so young insisting on speaking with the manager was not a regular occurrence; so the teller, with a smile on her face, went to ask the bank manager if he would speak with Michael, which, out of curiosity at the boldness and determination of the young boy, he agreed to do.

When Michael explained why he needed the new bicycle, the man decided that such an industrious young lad should be encouraged, and he instructed the teller to open a savings account for Michael and to ensure that his bankbook was kept up to date for him. From that day forward, all his money went into the account, and within a few more months, he was able to purchase a new bicycle for his deliveries.

One Sunday morning, during Michael's second year in high school, his father died suddenly of a heart attack. Michael's mother now found herself a widow with two young teenagers to raise alone and the added expense of a funeral. Michael realized that some of his newspaper route and pharmacy delivery savings would be needed for the funeral expenses, so he went out and got an even larger newspaper route to increase his income and help his mother with the new funeral bills.

After finishing high school, Michael decided that he would attend St. Patrick's College. During the summer break, to pay for his education, he worked on a road paving crew from dawn until dusk. The remuneration for the difficult and long hours of this job provided him with the money necessary for his tuition and his books, as well as enough left over to continue helping with the family's monthly bills. He continued to work on paving crews during his summer breaks until he began working for Dr. Forsey in his final year in college.

During his first year in college, his mother, a hard worker to the core, was still working cleaning offices at night to support Michael and his sister. Seeing the toll this was taking on her health, Michael talked to her about the necessity for her to give up some of this work before it adversely affected her health to the point that she end up in hospital. She resisted this decision until Michael announced that he would quit college if she continued on this path. Realizing that he was serious about quitting school, Mrs. O'Farrell finally agreed to leave some of the nightly work that she did, and Michael continued and completed his education, graduating with a Bachelor of Commerce degree.

After graduation, he started looking for work and found his way to the Department of Justice and into my life.

Chapter 3

Michael was a truly remarkable man, but I don't believe that he ever realized just how remarkable he was. I didn't either, until a day in late December of 1994, when, one evening after nearly thirty years of marriage, Michael handed me a letter and asked me to read it as he sat with me. As I read his words, my heart broke in two for him. The letter described the sexual abuse he had suffered for a number of years from a young boy when he joined the Boy Scouts until he was old enough and strong enough to be left alone. This news was a shock, but in some ways, the penny dropped on so many things that I had not been able to understand about him. Suddenly, all these things made perfect sense. We sat together and talked for a long while, and the following day, Michael decided that it was time he gave some thought to what, if anything, he could do to bring Gerald Joseph McGrath, his Boy Scout leader and abuser, to justice after so many years.

Michael began by preparing a file in which he placed a photo of McGrath and a list of the times, places, and years of abuse he had suffered under him, along with any documents he could find related to the traveling they had done together to the Boy Scouts Jamboree, as well as other journeys.

On one of the trips, McGrath had taken Michael to Saint John, New Brunswick, to meet his family. McGrath's brother was a police officer, and the man's wife, being very astute, noticed something in Michael that she had seen before and that worried her. So she took him aside during the visit and asked him if anything was wrong and if he was okay. McGrath had convinced Michael that should he tell anyone what was going on, both of them would be sent to jail. Being just a young lad, under such difficult circumstances, this threat came to the fore, and Michael said nothing was wrong. He wove all these things into a story that would eventually become his victim impact statement. Not only had Gerald McGrath been his Boy Scout leader, but he had also been his swim coach and hockey coach—all jobs that pedophiles use to find their numerous hapless victims.

As an adult now, Michael knew from everything he had read in various newspaper articles over the years about pedophiles, that these vermin never stop abusing children; and he was sure that he couldn't have been the first or last of McGrath's victims. In researching McGrath, Michael discovered that he had been tried in 1984, where he had pleaded guilty to eight counts of sexual assault. He had abused eight eleven- and twelve-year-old boys over a period of eight months. Because the judge felt sorry for him due to the fact that his lawyer very skillfully played up that "the offenses had occurred during a traumatic period in McGrath's life," the judge gave him a suspended sentence and placed him on three years' probation, in other words, a virtual "get out of jail free" card for a pedophile.

Michael's research into McGrath's past took up a great deal of his time and unearthed several other cases of sexual abuse for which McGrath had been tried. Why this man was continually rereleased from prison and still walking around free, breathing valuable air is a mystery to me. As a result of the research and Michael's determination to leave no stone unturned, it was two years before he felt that he had accumulated enough evidence to take to the police.

In May of 1996, he went to the police department with the documents he had amassed in his file and spoke with an officer there. Several times over the next three years, Michael called the police officer to inquire about the progress of the case. He was continually told that "these things take time." Finally, in March of 1999, he decided that he had waited long enough, so he went back to the police department to ask what was being done about his complaint.

Fortunately, he brought with him a copy of all the information he had given to the officer with whom he had met in 1996.

He was told that the police officer who had dealt with him couldn't meet with him as he was working on another case at the moment and probably wouldn't be able to see him for several days. Assuming that there would be a file on record and that any officer could check it and let him know what was happening, he asked to see someone else. He was shown to a different office and asked to wait. A different police officer, Sgt. Dave Shea, soon entered the room and asked Michael the reason for his visit. Michael went on to explain that he had made a complaint in 1996 and gave Sgt. Shea the name of the person who had dealt with him. Michael said that he was wondering why he had heard nothing about his complaint for three years. Upon checking the files, Sgt. Shea immediately asked Michael what he expected the police department to do since the file that had been opened about his complaint had nothing in it. Then, Michael opened up the briefcase he had brought with him, took out all the information he had given the previous police officer, and laid it on the desk. As Sgt. Shea looked over the information, Michael could see that he was becoming quite angry. He asked Michael if he wouldn't mind waiting a few minutes. Then, leaving his office door open, he went down the hall to another office, and Michael could hear him chastising the first officer for his laziness and dereliction of duty in neglecting Michael's complaint of such egregious abuse and leaving him hanging for three years without doing any work on the file at all. We later learned that the first officer who had ignored Michael's complaint left the force shortly after and moved to the United States.

When Sgt. Shea returned, he apologized to Michael for the lack of progress on the file and said that he would personally and immediately start work on Michael's complaint. Within a very short time, thanks to Sgt. Shea's dedicated work, McGrath was charged.

The crown attorney, Brian Holowka, who had been given Michael's case to try, met with Michael and told him that he had reviewed the file and that because the offenses had happened so long ago, it was considered a historical case and one that would be very hard to win. The trial was set to begin in October 2000. It should have taken place earlier. However, after being charged, McGrath and his lawyer delayed the case for twelve months before entering a plea.

After the trial, Mr. Holowka told Michael that, one night, when he had been at home preparing his opening statement, his three-year-old son had come to him and climbed up on his knee. As he looked at the child, he tried to picture what the boy would be like when he reached the age of joining the Boy Scouts and what would happen to him if he were put in the hands of another McGrath. He then decided that this case was one he was going to win, no matter what, or how long ago the offenses had taken place.

On the day of the trial, McGrath kept his eyes on the floor, trying to appear pitiful, pious, and hurt at the allegations made by Michael. McGrath's attorney tried to convince the judge that the abuse suffered by Michael couldn't have had too much of a deleterious effect on him, given that he had had such a successful life and career.

Fortunately, the judge, Justice J. M. Bordeleau, was not impressed with this stance and informed the court that he had read Michael's victim impact statement three times, and although it would not now be necessary, Michael could, if he so wished, read his statement to the court.

Michael decided he did want to read his statement as he wanted people to know how pedophiles operate and how important it is to listen to children when they say they need help and not give them useless advice as he had been given by his parish priest shortly after the serious abuse had begun. He also wanted people to know that it is possible to have a good life despite this kind of abuse. It will be hard, and at times very hard, but it is possible to achieve and very much worth making the necessary effort to do so.

On October 26, 2000, McGrath was found guilty of all charges and given a sentence of four years in prison, which was added to the two years he had already been serving in New Brunswick since August 2000 arising from another sexual abuse conviction. The four-year sentence in Michael's case had been one of the longest sentences ever given in a historical case that had happened so long ago.

After McGrath was removed from the court and carted off to jail, Michael and I invited Brian Holowka and Dave Shea, who had followed through with the case, to join us and our family at an Italian restaurant, Il Garage, to celebrate. Both men accepted our invitation and joined us at the restaurant for a wonderful Italian dinner followed by tiramisu for dessert.

Chapter 4

The sexual abuse Michael suffered at the hands of Gerald McGrath had started when he joined the Boy Scouts. Michael's father thought that the Boy Scouts would be a good outlet for a young lad with the energy and interest in sports that Michael had. Unfortunately, no one knew about Gerald McGrath's tendencies, or, if they did, they did nothing about them. As with all pedophiles, they portray themselves as charming, kind people only interested in what's best for the children in their charge. The snake in the Garden of Eden could learn lessons about charm from these vermin.

At any rate, McGrath insinuated himself into the family, and as time went on, Michael's father realized that McGrath was not what he appeared to be. Michael overheard several heated arguments between his parents about McGrath whenever his father insisted that his contact with Michael be curbed and monitored. Sadly, during these arguments, Mrs. O'Farrell believed that Gerry, as he wanted to be called, was being unfairly maligned and refused to accept what Joe, Michael's father, was saying.

After Joe's sudden death, McGrath offered to move in with the family so that he could help Mrs. O'Farrell with the rent and other family expenses. Now, suddenly finding herself a widow with a funeral to arrange and two young, now fatherless, teenagers, Mrs. O'Farrell was in no state to understand what was happening and accepted McGrath's offer to help. Within days, McGrath moved into the apartment and right into Michael's bedroom. As the apartment only had three bedrooms, one for Mrs. O'Farrell, one for Kathy, and one for Michael, he had to share his with McGrath. This bedroom arrangement, of course, allowed McGrath to abuse Michael whenever he wanted to, and Michael had nowhere to go to stop it.

During this time, Michael, being a good Roman Catholic boy, was an altar boy during mass at the local church. In his naivete, he believed that if he told the parish priest during his confession about what was going on, the priest would do something to help him. Unfortunately, as is now commonly known, the Roman Catholic Church has no interest in pursuing or punishing pedophiles who abuse young boys. In fact, many of its own priests have proved to be some of the worst offenders, constantly shielded by the church and moved from parish to parish when a complaint is made about any one of them.

When Michael told the priest what was happening, the latter simply told him to "stay away from" his abuser! How can you stay away from someone with whom you share a bedroom? As I mentioned earlier, McGrath had been threatening Michael by telling him that if he told his mother or went to the police, both of them would be sent to jail because, at this time in history, homosexuality was considered a crime punishable by incarceration, and there would be no one left to help his mother. McGrath did not mention, of course, that sexual abuse was a serious offense with jail for the perpetrators—not the victims.

At the young age of fourteen, Michael had no way of understanding how good pedophiles are at manipulating and trying to convince their victims that they, too, are homosexual as a way of preventing them from going to the authorities. This threat ensured Michael's complete silence to his mother, the police, and everyone else for over forty years.

As Michael grew into a man and especially after he began working in the federal government, there was no way he wanted anyone to know about his abuse—especially not me. He never wanted to be pitied and thought of as a victim. Because he had been so young and vulnerable when the abuse began, he seemed at times to believe he was weak. And I believe, he often looked upon himself that way. He seemed unable to fully accept that, given what he had accomplished despite the egregious abuse he had endured, he was, in fact, the exact opposite of weak. I'm still at a loss to understand what gave him the courage to finally tell me, but I am eternally thankful that he did or he never would have been able to put the past and McGrath in their proper places—McGrath in jail and Michael finally free from this painful secret.

Chapter 5

During our fifty-six years together, Michael and I were blessed with three sons, Robert, James, and David. Our Robert lives here in Ottawa and is a music teacher and a professional musician as well as a professional residential painter. James lives in New Brunswick and is an elementary school teacher, and our youngest son, David, despite having dyslexia, was an expert in computer cybersecurity until his death at age thirty-eight in 2009 from lung cancer, the same insidious disease that has now taken my Michael.

David's diagnosis and death that year, in only eight short months, came as a severe shock to our whole family but especially to our two granddaughters, who were quite young at the time and who had loved their big, strong, happy Uncle David without reservation. In order to make peace with his loss, they decided that the reason David had to go was because he was so strong that God needed him to help hold up the stars—a fitting epitaph for their much loved uncle. Even though I love our David and miss him, especially on his birthday, at annual family celebrations, and when I hear someone speak his name, I have been able, to some extent, to incorporate his loss into my life. However, the loss of my Michael is a much different story.

To say that I miss Michael excruciatingly every minute of every day and long to be with him is a gross understatement. There are days when my heart physically aches at the loss of him. For me, the mornings are the worst parts of the day probably because our morning routine, after I retired in 2010, had been to go each day to the neighborhood restaurant, Al's Diner, and have breakfast together.

Michael was diagnosed with stage 4 terminal lung cancer in March of 2019, just a few months shy of the universe being virtually closed down due to COVID-19.

In the midsummer of 2018, prior to his diagnosis, Michael had noticed that he was losing weight rather rapidly. He went to our family physician, who had treated us for over thirty years, and said that he was worried about this sudden and rapid weight loss and asked about having a CT scan. Michael and I had had to deal with a very difficult family matter early in the spring, which had caused us both concern, and the doctor told Michael that the weight loss was most likely just a result of stress from the family situation.

Now, in Canada, the only province where a person can request and pay for certain services, including CT scans, is the province of Quebec. In all other provinces, the patient must get a referral from his/her doctor for these procedures that are done in a hospital and paid for by our provincial health-care insurance.

By the fall, as he continued to lose weight, especially in his muscles, he saw the doctor on another occasion and again asked if she would recommend a CT scan just to make sure there was nothing else going on. But, she continued to say that the weight loss was caused by the stress and didn't try to arrange for a CT scan for Michael until some time in October or November.

After waiting several weeks, we contacted the hospital to ask when the CT scan would take place. We were informed that the request for the scan was being triaged, and as the doctor had not given it any urgency, the request had been put at the bottom of the pile, and when they got around to it, he would be notified.

We waited and waited, and finally in early March with no scan on the horizon, Michael decided that he had waited long enough. So we contacted a clinic in Montreal, Quebec, and we were told we could go down the next day for the scan, which we did. After the procedure, at the end of the day, we received the devastating news that Michael had lung cancer in stage 4 and that it was terminal.

We came home and notified our doctor of the diagnosis. She immediately referred him to an oncologist for treatment. When Michael told the oncologist about his weight loss, especially in his muscles, the doctor told him that losing weight in the muscles was one of the first and earliest signs of cancer and should have been taken more seriously. We often asked ourselves later whether his disease could have been caught at an earlier, perhaps curable, stage had he simply been sent for the CT scan when he had first asked for one. By the time the hospital, where the CT scan had been requested, finally got back to us with an appointment, Michael had already been in treatment for his disease for over two months.

Prior to Michael's cancer, only twice in all the years that we were together can I recall him ever being physically ill. Once was in the mid-1970s during the Norwalk virus pandemic. The first person in our family to come down with the virus was our David, who was about four years old at the time. He was also the first to recover, and I can still remember him running from one of us to another carrying an empty Kentucky Fried Chicken bucket and bringing it to each of us in turn as our stomachs began to turn over. Even Michael was not spared throwing up.

The second time he was ill was a couple of years prior to his diagnosis when we both came down with the winter flu, despite us both having received the flu vaccine.

During Michael's chemotherapy and, eventually, his immunotherapy treatments, the only enjoyment he had was going for breakfast. While on chemotherapy, which many times brought him to his knees, he was also afflicted on a number of occasions by shingles in his eye, an ailment from which he had suffered almost yearly for over thirty years. During the early years of his affliction with shingles, each time he had a bout of the disease, doctors would take a sample from one of the sores and send it for testing as they could not believe how often the shingles was recurring as it usually happens only once or twice in a person's lifetime—not every year for thirty years. The results were always positive for shingles. Michael could simply never get a break from this misery.

When the chemotherapy stopped working, Michael was started on immunotherapy. Within a few weeks of starting this new regimen, he began developing large painful bleeding sores in his mouth as a result of the medications. These continued and worsened for a number of weeks until doctors finally prepared a medication that they called magic mouthwash, a compounded medication that immediately started to cure the sores. Why they didn't simply give him this medication at the beginning, I'll never know. Since mouth sores are a common painful occurrence for patients undergoing immunotherapy, why not give them the most potent medication at the beginning instead of telling them to try salt water and other useless things that never work and only allow the sores to get much worse, leaving patients suffering unnecessarily and unable to eat?

For Michael, who had been so healthy and strong during so much of his adult life, the fact that he was now feeling his strength dissipating each day, especially during the final months and weeks of his illness, was very difficult for him.

In the late fall of 2021, his weakness had become so serious that he was no longer able to walk without the aid of a walker, and within days, even with my help, he could barely make it up the stairs. So in early December, we ordered a stairlift for him, but due to the difficulties in transportation and delivery as a result of the COVID-19 virus, the lift didn't arrive until the first week in February, so Michael only had the benefit of it for a few weeks before he left.

Finally, after a determined, hard-fought three-year battle with this insidious disease, Michael's soul left this earth and joined our son David in heaven on Wednesday, March 16, 2022, two months shy of his eighty-first birthday. During the last weeks of his illness, I had moved Michael from our bedroom on the second floor of the house to a hospital bed in our bright west-facing living room on the first floor from where he could see the setting sun, and I was sleeping on the couch next to the bed.

From the onset of Michael's illness, I spent countless hours praying for his recovery. In fact, the place on the living room rug where I knelt to pray became flattened from the imprint of my knees. But sadly, it was to no avail as Michael's illness progressed until it took him. I believe that he had accomplished whatever it was that God sent him down here to do and it was time for him to return to heaven, from where he had come.

On the eve of the night Michael left, I was watching him sleep and listening to him breathe. For the previous couple of weeks, his breathing had been quite noisy with his inhalations sounding very congested and his exhalations eerily quiet with almost no sound at all. For the previous day, he had not spoken and spent almost all the time asleep. It was about 9:00 p.m. as I watched and listened.

Suddenly Michael opened his eyes wide and started looking at the ceiling. I could tell by the movement of his eyes that he was watching something happening up there, and it wasn't the ceiling he was seeing. All of a sudden, with a loud, clear voice he said, "*Oh*, it's so beautiful! It's *so* beautiful!" He continued watching the ceiling for another minute or so, and then he called up, "Hello, up there. Hello, up there." Within another minute, he was once again asleep. These were his last words, and he never again woke up. Michael had seen heaven where he was going and he was looking forward to it and he wasn't afraid. I think about this miracle and thank God almost every day for how lucky I was to be there in the room to be able to hear and watch Michael see where his new life would begin.

During the week that Michael left, our son Bob and his partner Brigitte had been staying with us, and Bob often held Michael's hand when the latter was awake. Michael had told Bob that he couldn't leave this earth unless Bob was there.

At this time, Bob was working on a painting contract that needed to be finished by the end of the week. As the days progressed, he told his father that he would soon need to go back to work but that he would stay until it was time for Michael to go and that it was okay for him to leave whenever he chose to do so.

On the morning of March 16, I awoke at three thirty and noticed that the room was quiet. In my sleep, I had become quite used to the rhythm of his breathing and, I believe, that the extended quietness in the room is what had awakened me. I went over to Michael. I felt him, and he was warm, but when I placed my ear to his chest, I heard no heartbeat—Michael was gone. I immediately called upstairs to Bob and Brigitte to tell them that Michael had passed. Bob, too, had just awoken at three thirty.

Later on that morning, I called Michael's sister and told her that Michael had passed at 3:30 a.m., and she told me that she, too, had awakened at three thirty. After speaking with Kathy, the next person on my list to call was my good friend Lyla, who had been my proverbial "shoulder to cry on" when I had called her crying each morning as I walked our dog, Maya. I told her that Michael had passed at three thirty. She also had awakened at three thirty. All I could think of was that Michael was telling all the people close to him that he was leaving on his way to his new adventure.

Now comes the reason for my writing this book.

Chapter 6

Several weeks after Michael left, I decided to go to the Chapters bookstore to look for any new books I could find on near-death experiences. While I have a library room that contains about ten or more different books on this subject, I am always on the lookout for new ones. I found two new ones at Chapters and also noticed another book, on a different shelf, entitled *Signs: The Secret Language of the Universe*. As I already had two new books in my arms, as well as my purse, I decided to pass up on this third book, but on my way to the pay counter, something made me go back and get it.

When I got home, I decided, as a treat, to start to read one of the new books. Getting myself a good hot cup of tea, I sat on the sofa and looked at the three titles. For some reason, the title of the third book intrigued me, and I decided to read that one first.

Signs: The Secret Language of the Universe was written by Laura Lynne Jackson, a psychic medium from the United States. On page 12 of her book, she talks about how each one of us has a "team of light," a group of souls on the other side made up of the "God energy,…which is the highest and most powerful source of love,… our spirit guides/the angelic realm," and "…our loved ones who have crossed over." In an interview I saw of her on television, she suggested that we ask our loved ones to send us what will be their sign to indicate that they are connecting with us.

One day, just after reading *Signs*, I was driving to church for a quiet visit with God, and on my way, I asked Michael a question to which I desperately needed the answer "yes". I had tried to come up with a sign for him to send me when he wanted to connect with me, but I had been unable to come up with one that would stick. Michael had loved the red cardinal birds and always answered back to the males when he heard them calling in the morning. I thought that perhaps the cardinal would be a good sign, but somehow, it didn't feel right.

At any rate, while I was driving to the church and asking Michael for a sign, the words *pink elephant* popped into my mind. From where, I had no idea. No elephant of any color had any connection with Michael or me, but that was what popped into my mind—a pink elephant! I couldn't believe that this could be a sign, but I said to Michael, "Okay, if your answer to my question is yes, you need to send me a pink elephant!" As you can probably imagine, the chances of my seeing a pink elephant were so astronomical as to be impossible to calculate, but a pink elephant was what I needed to see. So I resigned myself to never getting the answer I sought and trying to come up with another sign that could possibly work.

During the previous week and a half, both Bob and Brigitte had been staying with me because of a severe storm that hit the city on May 21, causing enormous, severe damage and electricity blackouts all over the city because of downed power lines. The storm had badly affected their area, with the power out everywhere. In the evening on this particular Tuesday, they wanted to walk down to the village to have a veggie burger that Bob had recently enjoyed at a restaurant called Churchill's. They asked me to accompany them, but I was tired and had already eaten and really wasn't in the mood to go out. However, as the weather was fine, at their urging, I decided to go and at least have a cup of coffee.

When we entered the restaurant, I noticed that there was a long bar that ran down the wall on the right, and in the open area on the left were several individual tables with patrons, some eating and others chatting and waiting for their meals. A pleasant server came over to us, and Bob said that we would like to eat out on the roof patio above the restaurant. The server said that it would only take her a few minutes to clear a table and for us to wait there and she would return.

As I looked around the restaurant, my eyes drifted to the bar. I looked down the length of it and saw at the end a wall with a beautiful large thick dark-brown door. As I raised my eyes above it, I almost collapsed. Above the door was a lighted pink neon elephant! How I managed to stay upright and not collapse and let on that something momentous had happened, I do not know. I had told no one about my conversation with Michael and did not intend to do so now. For me, the only explanation for the pink elephant was that Michael knew how desperately I needed an answer to my question, and he also, somehow, knew that Bob and Brigitte would be going to a restaurant that had a pink elephant neon sign on the wall!

That was the first and most important sign for me that Michael is still in my life and that I can communicate with him. There have been other occasions when he has answered my questions, and I'll tell you about them below. But first I must go back a bit in time.

Chapter 7

On the Thursday before Michael left, I called his sister Kathy to tell her that Michael would not be with us much longer. She told me that she had intended to call me that day because she had some news about her husband John who was only a year or two older than Michael. The news was not good.

John had hurt his back in late December caused, he thought, by pulling a muscle by doing some strenuous vacuuming. Knowing he had an appointment for a physical in mid-January, Kathy rubbed liniment on his back and gave him Tylenol to take care of the pain until his appointment. John had several ailments that had been plaguing him for a number of years, all of which were under control by various medications. However, this back pain was something new.

When John went for his doctor's appointment, the doctor said that he wanted to have an x-ray taken of John's back as well as a CT scan to learn if there was something other than a pulled muscle causing his discomfort. When the results of the scan came back in early March, they showed that John was suffering from bone cancer throughout his body. The doctor told Kathy that John would not be going home from the hospital; he would, instead, need to be transferred for special care to a palliative care residence.

Unfortunately—or perhaps, fortunately—John never made it to the palliative care residence as his soul left this world on March 21, just five days after Michael's departure. In only one week, Kathy had lost not only her brother but her husband as well.

A week after Michael's death, Bob and I decided that we would hold his celebration of life memorial in late spring or early summer.

We decided on June 11 as the day. In the intervening time, I had a DVD prepared with pictures of Michael from when he was a young child up until just prior to his illness, which would be shown on a computer screen during the memorial. I also accumulated several paper photos of Michael to be displayed around the rooms.

Like Michael and me, John and Kathy had also lost a child. Their loss was severe in that their little girl, Lynne, died of sudden infant death syndrome at only a few weeks of age in 1964, just days prior to Michael's starting work at the Combines Investigation Branch.

I decided that, at Michael's memorial, I wanted to talk about John and Lynne. I practiced a short speech in which I mentioned that Michael and John, both fathers, were now happy and healthy and enjoying spending time with their children whom they had not seen in years and that this was how people should try to remember them.

I practiced this speech over and over and decided that before I said anything, I needed to get Michael's approval that this was what he wanted me to do. So I asked him to send me an elephant; it could be a picture, someone saying the word, or anything connected to "elephant"—that was what he needed to send to let me know that he approved of my plan and that he would help me to get through my little speech without breaking down.

Three days before Michael's memorial, I had obtained the paper proof from our provincial government that I had received all my vaccinations against COVID-19, including the fourth shot, the second booster, and I decided to bring it to the Staples store where I knew that they could reduce it and laminate it back to back to a copy of my driver's license in the size of a credit card that would fit into my wallet. I gave the document to the technician, and she said that it would take a few minutes. I decided to look around the store.

I went up and down a couple of aisles, and on my second pass, I looked to my right, and there on a shelf near the bottom of the unit was a gray plastic elephant scotch tape dispenser with the tip of the elephant's trunk as the cutting end! There it was, my sign from Michael that he approved of my speech.

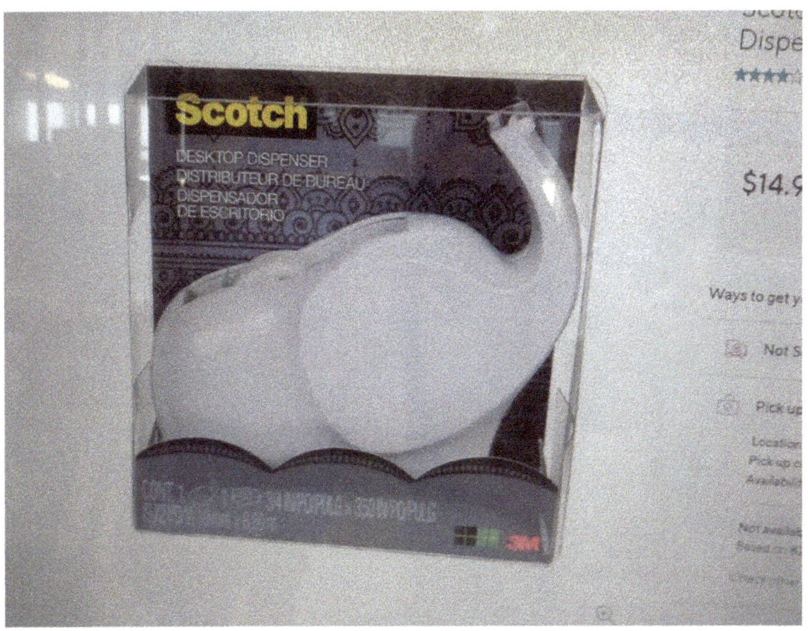

At Michael's memorial, near the end of the time slot, I asked attendees to wait for a few minutes because I had something I wanted to say. I began by thanking them for coming to celebrate Michael's life. Then, I talked about the miracle of Michael seeing heaven, and I ended with words about John, Lynne, Michael, and our David. I do not know how my words affected them; I can only hope that they will remember Michael's miracle and that both he and John are healthy and happy and that this is how they should be remembered. Several people have written to say that the memorial was well done.

After the memorial, Bob, Brigitte, and I headed for home. During the ride, I said that I hoped Michael had found his memorial matched his personality and helped people to remember him and his amazing determination and strength. A few minutes into the drive, we had to stop at a red light in the downtown area, which was the Vietnamese part of the city. As I looked around at gaily dressed people crossing the street, my eyes were suddenly drawn to a wall directly in front of the car—on it was a gigantic mural of an elephant all decorated with colored tassels and filling over half of the entire wall! Michael had obviously enjoyed his memorial.

A week ago, I wanted to send some financial support to two charities that I have wanted to help for several years but had not as yet done. I decided that I would send each of them a donation, and I reminded Michael how I always feel that we, here in Canada, are so fortunate to live in such a wonderful country that we should be willing, if able, to help those not so lucky and that I wanted to help out. I asked him to send me a sign that he approved of this decision and the amounts I was going to donate. Sure enough, a couple of hours later as I watched television, what should pop up on the screen but a photo of an elephant in a commercial for an upcoming program! Off went the letters and cheques to the two charities.

One of my most recent requests from Michael was how he would feel about my writing a book about his journey. I asked once again for a sign, and as I was watching the program *60 Minutes*, a photo of an elephant logo appeared. It is a symbol for one of the political parties in the United States, can't remember which one. But as it was quite a small picture, I asked Michael to send me something a bit more visible—boy, did he ever! An hour or so later, he sent me two huge photos of elephants in TV commercials that covered most of the screen. Hence, this book.

As I said earlier, I doubt that Michael ever knew what a truly talented and remarkable person he was. Despite the years of sexual abuse he suffered as a young boy and teenager, he managed to get a university education, have a very successful marriage, and in his employment at the Department of Justice, rose to become the Director of the Combines Investigation Branch, with two hundred lawyers, economists, and other employees under his direction until he retired in the mid-1980s.

After he retired from the public service, he started two businesses, one a consulting firm where, given his extensive experience with the law, he often did contract work with the Combines Investigation Branch, and the other, a retail business called Imagine Ocean, selling aquariums and tropical fish.

As a young teenager, Michael had kept freshwater fish and had learned how to keep them healthy and thriving. In this new business, he would need to learn all about saltwater fish that are difficult to keep as both the pH and salt levels of the water have to be closely monitored. Within two years, Michael had learned so much about saltwater fish that many of his customers called him the fish doctor, and customers from other aquarium stores often came to him for advice on what to do when their fish were sick.

We had opened the store in the late fall of 1989. During that summer, rumors had been circulating about a new goods and services tax the federal government was considering on implementing. Sure enough, in January 1991, the federal goods and services tax (GST) at the rate of 7 percent came into effect. This was added to the provincial sales tax of 8 percent, for a total tax of 15 percent on all goods bought and sold from the store.

When Michael opened the store, the amount of profit he had hoped to make was 7 percent, so the new GST removed any hope of a profit from this new business. Given this new reality, it was necessary for him to use some of the earnings from his consulting business to help float the store.

After a couple of difficult years with no profit, Michael decided that when the lease for the premises came up for renewal at the five-year mark, he would not renew it and would, instead, close the business. However, when the lease came up for renewal, our sole employee wanted to take over the store instead of closing it, so Michael let him have the business at cost.

Michael excelled at everything to which he turned his hand. He became a very good landscape artist; he learned how to work with stained glass and produced several beautiful windows for friends. He learned how to work with ceramic tile and tiled the walls in both bathrooms in our home from floor to ceiling. In fact, his tile work was so precise that a man we hired to tile the bathroom floors asked Michael if he was an engineer because the wall tiling had been so professionally and perfectly done. He even designed and built a two-tiered deck off our patio door in the dining room. Simply everything he did was done carefully, expertly, and professionally.

As is obvious by now, I ask Michael for a sign whenever I need an answer to a particular question. But he is not the only one who sends me signs. It might interest you to know about the signs that I receive from our David; but when they started to appear, I didn't know that I could simply just ask for one.

I would now like to tell you a bit about our David.

As I mentioned earlier, Michael and I had three sons. Our two oldest sons were granted the gene for music, but, unfortunately, although he absolutely loved music, our David was not favoured with this gift—instead, he received the gift of computer cyber analysis and code development. When it came to computers, David was the go-to guy that everyone called. He even developed a program that was later patented. Even during the severity of his cancer treatments in hospital, it was not unusual for members of his team to come to his room with a coding problem that no one but David could solve.

Our David had a wonderful love of animals—all of them. He and his wife Amanda always kept dogs and often cats as well, and David had a large salt water aquarium full of tropical salt water fish, the love of which he developed while working in Michael's pet shop. When his favourite greyhound dog, Doonie, developed cancer, he spent countless hours researching medical articles from reputable sites on the internet trying to find anything that could help her and extend her life.

Unfortunately, in her case, as well as it would turn out to be in David's a few years later, there really was no way to help Doonie. David was devastated at her loss. To David, as it is to most of us who have pets, the animals become members of our family—they are no longer just furry, scaly creatures, they are amazing souls with feelings, wants, needs and desires—just like ours.

I sincerely hope that when David was at heaven's door, Doonie was there wagging her tail to welcome him and that since that time he has been playing ball and Frisbee as often as he wants to with Doonie and all his other pets who are gone there now.

A few weeks after David left us, I awoke in the middle of the night feeling myself being squeezed with a big bear hug—but it wasn't coming from Michael. Michael was sound asleep beside me.

David knew that my absolutely favourite creature in the universe is the monarch butterfly. As I have said, David left us almost fourteen years ago now, on December 21, 2009. In May 2010, on the first Mother's Day after he left, when I opened my morning newspaper, there, on the left-hand side of the paper taking up half the page, was a giant photo of a monarch butterfly. And, on my seventy-second birthday, in December 2018, I once again opened the newspaper to find a half-page photo of a monarch.

As this was only a few weeks prior to Michael's diagnosis, I sometimes wonder if this was David's way of letting me know that some change in our lives was coming and that he would be there when we needed him. Now every time I see any butterfly, I say "hi" to both David and Michael.

Chapter 8

As I mentioned in the last chapter, we lost our David a few days before Christmas in 2009. Michael and I and David's widow, Amanda, decided to have David's celebration of life memorial in the early spring of 2010.

We began to accumulate various photos of David to put on display in the venue, and Michael even had three photos enlarged to two by three feet and laminated to a particle board. There were also some photos of David on slides that we wanted to be shown on a computer screen. These photos were in a two-inch by four-inch by half-inch-sized slide case.

About a day or two before David's memorial, we decided to put everything for the memorial together in one place so nothing would be forgotten. We stacked the three large laminated photos against the sofa in the living room and put the other photos on the pillows. Then we went to put the slide case beside these. But we couldn't find it. Michael thought I had it, and I thought he did. So we began to search for it. We knew we had last seen the case in the office, so we went there to start the search.

We checked out the tops of the two desks in the room, opened all their drawers, and came up empty. No slide case could we find. We opened all the drawers in the filing cabinet thinking that perhaps in our dazed state, we had inadvertently put the case in there without thinking. We searched and we searched and we searched again to no avail. Finally, in my desperation, I decided to ask David to help us find the slides, and then we left the office.

After about ten minutes, something made me go back to the office and to one of the two desks in particular. This desk had a stack of letter-sized pages in one corner propped against the back of the desk and leaning on the wall. Something made me start shuffling through the papers, and there in the middle of the stack at the bottom of one of the pages was the slide case. I thanked David and made a mental note of this event and kept it safely in the back of my mind.

Several months later, one evening in late October, Michael and I went to check on the house of an elderly friend of ours named Robert, who spent several winter months each year in the United Kingdom. He had given us an expandable cardboard file folder secured with a large elastic containing the key to the house, the insurance policy, the number of the security code, etc. After checking the house, setting the security apparatus, and locking the door, we headed for home.

As we were parking the car in the driveway, Michael's cell phone rang. He had the file folder in his hand as he exited the car and answered the call. He put the file folder on the roof of the car while he spoke. As the call ended, before going inside, we decided that as we had been busy all day, we would go to Al's Diner for a quick supper.

By this time of day in October, it is fairly dark, and it had been raining quite hard off and on all day and had been very windy. This particular day was garbage day for recycling of papers, cardboard, grass clippings, etc. All the neighborhood garbage bins were out on the sidewalks and the lawns, and sidewalks and roads were covered with several layers of wet, dirty leaves that had been blown down by the strong winds.

After returning home from our dinner, we went into the house, and I asked Michael to give me the file to be put back in the filing cabinet. We both somehow thought that one of us had brought the file into the house before going to the restaurant for supper, but after a thorough search, we realized that it wasn't there. Then Michael suddenly said, "Oh my God, I left it on the roof of the car! If anyone gets hold of that file, they could go through the house and steal everything in it. We have to find that file! Otherwise, we have to call

Robert in the UK, get hold of his insurance agent, get a new lock put on the door, and heaven knows what else we will need to do!"

So once again I said to David, "Please help us find that file. We really need to find it, or we will have a ton of trouble to take care of. We can't do so without your help."

So we set out in the rain hoping that by some miracle, we would find the file at the end of the laneway. Of course, it wasn't there, so we started to drive slowly down the street. The possibility of finding that file among the millions of dirty leaves was pretty remote. Michael was looking down both sides of the street, and I was looking down on the right side. Suddenly, Michael said, "There's something on the sidewalk right over there."

He stopped the car, and I got out. There, under a thick, dirty pile of leaves was a two-inch corner of the file sticking out. How Michael was able to see such a small piece of cardboard under the leaves in the dark and in the rain, I'll never know. The possibility of someone having seen the file and thinking it was just paper garbage and putting it in their recycling was very great. On the other hand, if a dishonest person had found it and realized what was inside, heaven only knows what would have happened. David had come to our rescue once again.

More recently, I once again had need of David's help. A few weeks after my Michael left, I needed to return a broken Cablevision box to Rogers at the mall a few blocks from our home. It was about eight thirty at night when I left for the mall. When I exited the car, I dropped my car keys, and they made a noise. I picked them up, put them in my pocket, and headed for the store to drop off the broken box. Then I headed home.

Now before Michael got ill, one of the last gifts he had given me was a beautiful key chain with a butterfly on it. I kept that key chain on a hook by the front door and simply grabbed it when I needed to take our dog, Maya, for a walk. When I got home, I parked the car in the garage, entered the house, put a leash on Maya, and went to the hook for the key. But, it wasn't there. I searched all my coat pockets in case I had worn a different coat when I last took her out, but I couldn't find it. I was devastated and brokenhearted at the thought that I had lost my last gift from Michael. Then, I thought, *Oh, my Lord, what if I had it in my pocket, it fell out when I dropped the car keys, and it's still in the parking lot at the mall?*

I drove back to the parking lot, but someone else was in the spot I had parked previously. I tried to look for the key, but it was so dark now that I really couldn't see properly. So I decided to wait until the following morning and go there early before the store opened and see if I could find it where I had left the car. I drove home, parked the car in the garage, and went into the house. This time, I asked both David and Michael to help me find the key.

I started, once again, going through all the pockets in my other jackets just in case I had missed it. But it wasn't there. Suddenly, I got the urge to go and look in the car. It was quite dark in the garage as one of the ceiling lights was out, so I took a little flashlight and opened the front passenger door—why that particular door, I don't know. Shining the light into the car, I saw something twinkling down between the two front seats—there it was, my key! How the key got there, I do not know. I don't recall taking it with me when I went to drop off the broken box. But there it was, stuck between the seats. I thanked both Michael and David profusely for helping me find my precious gift.

There is one more thing I would like to tell you. If you'll recall, when I first heard the words "pink elephant" pop into my head, I couldn't imagine why these words were to be Michael's sign.

On Saturdays and Sundays there is a farmer's market at the end of our street. Yesterday, being Saturday, I decided to go down to the market and just walk around. I noticed a new vendor there who was selling small cup-sized flower pots with tiny succulent plants in them. As I looked over the table, I came across an elephant planter and on its side was the design of a sunflower, which is one of my favourite flowers. So, I purchased it.

When I got home, I found a nice spot for it on my kitchen window sill. As I mused about the number of elephant signs Michael had sent me, I wondered why the elephant had become his sign, suddenly, it hit me—our David's widow, Amanda, loves elephants. They are her favourite animal in the whole world—and, she has a tattoo of an elephant on her ankle! There it was, the elephant connection closing the circle—not only connecting Michael to me, but also, in a way, connecting David and his widow, Amanda, too.

So as you can see, signs are not the only way our loved ones can communicate with us. They are always ready to help; all we need to do is ask. But we also need to believe that the help we get is actually from them and not just a coincidence or luck. These last two words are what people use when they do not want to think about the other side because it makes them focus on the fact that none of us will live forever—not even them. But in this way, they miss some of the most wonderful events in their lives, and they are much the poorer for it.

I truly hope that anyone who reads this story will realize that our loved ones who go on to their next life are still capable of connecting with us; we just have to ask and wait for a sign. You will miss their physical presence. As I have said, I miss Michael every minute of every day, but knowing where he is and that he is enjoying spending time with our David allows me to go on.

I would like to leave you with something that Dr. Elizabeth Kubler-Ross has said:

> Death is simply the shedding of the physical body like the butterfly shedding its cocoon. It is a transition to a higher state of consciousness where you continue to perceive, to understand, to laugh, and to be able to grow.

As the title of this book says, my Michael is not here; he is present elsewhere. One day I will be with him, and I look forward with anticipation to that time when I, too, will be "not here, present elsewhere."

About the Author

Mary O'Farrell is a retired public servant and grandmother whose manuscript here is her first foray into the world of writing. She is a lover of all kinds of stories, in particular those related to life after death, which has now been proven to her by her adored husband, Michael. She hopes that this book will be of help to all who are grieving the loss of a loved one and who are unafraid to look through the invisible curtain separating the visible, tangible world from the unseen world of the spirit.

9 798888 751575 55